New Readers Press

ReadingWise

Comprehension Strategies That Work

6

Series Consultant

Diane J. Sawyer, Ph.D.
Murfree Professor of Dyslexic Studies
Middle Tennessee State University

ReadingWise 6: Comprehension Strategies That Work
ISBN 1-56420-330-1
Copyright © 2003 New Readers Press
New Readers Press
Division of Proliteracy Worldwide
1320 Jamesville Avenue, Syracuse, New York 13210

Printed in the United States of America
9 8 7 6 5 4 3 2

All proceeds from the sale of New Readers Press materials
support literacy programs in the United States and worldwide.

Developer: Kraft & Kraft, New York, NY
Series Editor: Judi Lauber
Production Director: Heather Witt
Designer: Shelagh Clancy
Illustrations: Carolyn Boehmer, Luciana Mallozzi, Matt Terry, Linda Tiff
Production Specialist: Alexander Jones
Cover Design: Kimbrly Koennecke

Contents

To the Student

Welcome to *ReadingWise 6*. This book will help you understand and remember more of what you read.

Good readers think when they read. This book is about the thinking skills they use.

Life has already taught you a wide range of thinking skills. This book will show you how to use them for reading.

ReadingWise 6 has 31 lessons. Each lesson builds one skill and has four parts:

- This Is the Idea tells what skill you will learn.
- Take a Closer Look shows how to use the skill.
- Try It helps you use the skill.
- Use It lets you use the skill on your own.

Adults need to read many things every day. This book includes

- news and sports reports
- opinion columns
- charts and graphs
- ads
- rules and directions
- how-to tips
- tables of contents
- texts in history, science, nature, and language
- and other things

As you read these things, *ReadingWise* helps you practice thinking skills. And these skills help you become a better reader.

Using Clues to Meaning

A writer may define a word or use a synonym to explain it. Other clues in the text, combined with what you know, may help you guess what a word means. These are all *context clues*.

This Is the Idea

Read this part of a health text and decide what vertigo is.

Vertigo

Most people feel vertigo at one time or another. Perhaps as a child you would spin around quickly and enjoy the vertigo afterwards. For someone who feels vertigo when climbing a ladder, however, that dizziness can be dangerous.

What does *vertigo* mean? The writer says you may have felt vertigo after spinning around quickly. You know that spinning can make you dizzy, so you may guess that *vertigo* means "dizziness." In the next sentence, the writer uses *vertigo* and *dizziness* in the same way. These context clues help you figure out that *vertigo* means "dizziness."

Take a Closer Look

Read this sports article and decide what *spelunking* and *novice* mean.

Try Spelunking

If you're looking for a new adventure sport, try spelunking. But before you rush off to explore a cave, learn the safety rules. For one thing, don't go spelunking alone. Caves can be dangerous, and a novice spelunker will follow a spelunker who has training and experience.

Look for context clues:

- A cask is a barrel.
- a cask, which is a barrel
- a cask, or barrel,
- a cask, a barrel,
- the cask— the barrel—
- The wine was stored in round wooden casks made of oak.

Write your answers. *Hint:* Look for context clues in blue ink.

1. What is the sport of spelunking?

   _____

2. What is a novice spelunker?

   _____

Try It

Read this science text and decide what the terms in it mean.

How Glaciers Shaped the Land

As the great glaciers of the ice age melted, they left changes in the landscape that are still visible today. The eskers of New England, long winding ridges of gravel and sand, were deposited by rivers of meltwater. The southern half of Long Island is a vast moraine, a heap of sand, soil, and rock left behind as the glacier retreated.

Write your answers.

1. What is an esker?

   _____

2. What is meltwater?

   _____

3. What is a moraine?

   _____

Use It

Read this science text and decide what the terms in it mean.

Why Stars Twinkle

To our eyes, stars look like tiny points of light that twinkle in the night sky. This scintillation is caused by ripples in the air that refract the starlight. In other words, the ripples bend the light this way and that before it reaches our eyes. But the way stars look to us is deceptive. They are really huge balls of glowing gas.

Write your answers.

1. What does *refract* mean?

   _____

2. What does *scintillation* mean?

   _____

3. What does *deceptive* mean?

   _____

Deciding How to Read

◆ *Setting a Purpose and Method*

Before you start to read, think about *why* and *how* you are going to read. For example, you might read slowly to understand something in depth, or you might read quickly to find a fact or get the general idea.

This Is the Idea

Decide why and how you would read the rest of this sports feature.

Our Predictions

The new season is just about to get underway, and our sports columnists bring you their predictions in this issue. You'll find a chart with their predictions below. Beginning on page 3, they give you the detailed reasoning behind those predictions.

Sometimes you read quickly to get just the information you want. Suppose you just want to know what teams the columnists predict will do well. You will look at the chart and read it quickly. If you want details about the teams, you will turn to page 3 and read more slowly.

What to do

- To understand something in depth, read slowly.
- To find just the facts you need, read quickly.
- To help yourself remember, take notes.

Take a Closer Look

Decide why and how you would read chapters in this book.

Contents

Circle your answers.

1. Why would someone read Chapter 1 quickly?
   a. to find out what year radio and television were invented
   b. to understand exactly how broadcasting works

2. Why would someone read Chapter 4 slowly and carefully?
   a. to find out how many people use cell phones today
   b. to understand cell phone technology

Try It

Why and how would you read this special section of a newspaper?

New Car Supplement

It's that time of year again. The auto makers are releasing their new models. In this special section, you will find everything you want to know about the latest cars and trucks. You'll also find a handy comparison chart that will help you pick the vehicle that's right for you and your family.

Write your answers.

1. You want to find out which light trucks get the best gas mileage. Will you read this special section quickly or slowly?

_____

2. You want a new car, but you haven't made up your mind what kind to buy. Will you read this special section quickly or slowly?

_____

Use It

Decide why and how you would read the rest of this news report.

Parade Route Announced

SOUTHERN CITY — The annual Independence Day parade will be held next Saturday, and that means that parking will be prohibited along the parade route. (A map of the route, showing streets where parking is prohibited, appears on page 6.) The city's Independence Day parade has an interesting history.

Write your answers.

1. What is one reason you might have for turning to page 6?

_____

_____

2. You're interested in knowing how the parade got started and how it has grown over the years. What will you do?

_____

Asking the Right Questions

Asking questions about the text helps you understand what you read. Asking questions helps you identify the most important parts of the text.

This Is the Idea

As you read this science text, ask "What? Who? Why?"

The Comeback of the Bison

Before Europeans arrived in America, there were millions upon millions of wild bison (sometimes called buffalo). New settlers and hunters killed so many bison that by the middle of the 19th century there were fewer than 2,000 left. Today, thanks to efforts to protect them, there are hundreds of thousands of these animals.

As you read this text, you can find out what a bison is, who destroyed the great bison herds, and why bison made their comeback.

Take a Closer Look

As you read this parenting tip, ask "Who? What? Why?"

Teaching Children to Control *Anger*

We all get angry when things go wrong. Children often do not know how to keep their tempers under control. You can teach a child to follow a few simple steps when anger builds.

First, get into a relaxed position.
Second, take a deep breath, and another, and another.
Third, in your mind, tell yourself to calm down.

Ask yourself
- Who?
- What?
- When?
- Where?
- How?
- Why?

Write your answers.

1. What is one of the three steps that an angry child should follow?

_____

2. Who might find this article useful?

_____

Try It

As you read this science text, ask yourself questions.

Getty Images

Eclipses of the Sun and Moon

In an eclipse of the sun, the moon passes between the sun and the Earth, and the moon's shadow falls on the Earth. We see the moon hide the sun. In an eclipse of the moon, the Earth passes between the sun and the moon, and the Earth's shadow falls on the moon. If we were on the moon, we would see the Earth hide the sun.

Write your answers.

1. In an eclipse of the sun, what shadow falls on the Earth?

   _____

2. Why does an eclipse of the moon occur?

   _____

   _____

Use It

As you read this history text, ask yourself questions.

The Clasp-Locker

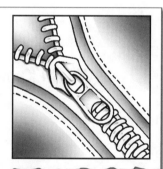

The clasp-locker was invented by Whitcomb Judson. In the late 19th century, Judson was looking for a quicker and easier way to fasten the high boots that people wore. Instead of long laces, he used two strips of metal hooks and eyes. A slide between the strips slipped the hooks into the eyes. Judson never managed to make a success of the clasp-locker, but after his death an improved version became the zipper.

Write your answers.

1. What was a clasp-locker?

   _____

2. Why did Judson invent the clasp-locker?

   _____

3. How did the clasp-locker fasten boots?

   _____

Checking as You Read

◆ *Monitoring Comprehension*

Use a chart to check your understanding as you read. Recall what you already know about the subject and decide what you would like to learn. As you read, keep track of what you learn.

This Is the Idea

Read the cover of this book and decide what it will be about.

You may or may not know the word *meteor.* Even so, from the title and picture you may guess that this book will be about space and about something that burns as it travels across the sky.

Take a Closer Look

Look at this chart about meteors, and decide what should go on it.

What I Know	What I Want to Know	What I Learned

1. Let's say that you already know this about meteors. Put it on the chart. **Meteors are rocks and most of them are very small.**

2. Let's say that you want to know this about meteors. Put it on the chart. **Why do they light up the way they do?**

Try It

What facts about meteors do you learn as you read this part of the book?

> Countless bits of rock, called meteoroids, orbit the sun in the same way that planets do. Most of them are extremely small, about the size of a grain of sand. When the Earth passes through a group of these meteoroids, they are drawn toward the planet by its gravity.
>
> As meteoroids approach the Earth's surface, they begin to fall through the air. Friction with the air causes them to heat up, and we may see them as fiery streaks rushing across the night sky. Some people call them "shooting stars," but they are not stars, but bits of rock heated by friction until they flare brightly. A meteoroid that falls through the air and glows is called a meteor.
>
> Some larger meteoroids—not very many—don't burn up completely and actually make it to the surface of the Earth. When they do, the rocks are called meteorites.

Add the things you learned to the chart in Take a Closer Look.

Use It

Read the cover of this book.

On separate paper, make a chart like the one in Take a Closer Look. Put on the chart what you know about starting a small business and what you want to know.

Find a book or article about starting a small business. Read enough to learn something you did not know. Add what you learned to the chart.

Putting It in a Few Words

◆ *Summarizing*

As you read, pause now and then to summarize what you have read by putting it into a few words. Summarizing can help you remember what you've read.

This Is the Idea

Read this part of a sports article and summarize it in your mind.

> ## The Sport of Curling
>
> To those who do not curl, the sport of curling looks like something made up on the spot as a joke. Players slide heavy stones down a rink of ice, trying to get the stones to coast into a goal marked on the ice. Oddest of all are the sweepers. They brush the ice with brooms to make the stones slide farther or to change their direction as they slide.

You could summarize the main points of this article in a few words. "In the sport of curling, players slide heavy stones across an ice rink toward a goal, and sweepers use brooms to affect how the stones slide."

To sum it up

- Decide which parts are most important.
- Put the most important parts into a few words.
- Don't include details that aren't very important.

Take a Closer Look

Read this part of a health text and summarize it in your mind.

> ## Caffeine
>
> Caffeine is found in coffee beans, tea leaves, cola nuts, and cacao beans and in the drinks made from those sources — coffee, tea, cola drinks, and hot chocolate. Caffeine acts as a stimulant on several parts of the body, including the nervous system, the heart muscle, and the lungs, which is why it makes your heart beat faster, your breathing shallower, and your hands a bit shaky.

Check two sentences that you would use if you summarized this text.

_____ a. Caffeine is found in coffee, tea, cola drinks, and hot chocolate.

_____ b. Caffeine stimulates several parts of the body.

_____ c. Caffeine makes your hands a bit shaky.

Try It

Read this part of a history text. Think about how you would sum it up.

State Songs

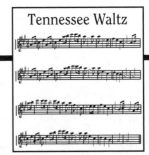

Tennessee Waltz

Almost every state in the Union has an official state song—at least one official state song. Three states have two official state songs, West Virginia has three, and Arkansas has four. Tennessee tops them all, though, with five official state songs, including "Tennessee Waltz" and "Rocky Top." Only New Jersey and Virginia have no official state song.

Circle the better summary of "State Songs."

a. Almost every state has an official state song, except Tennessee. It has five official state songs, including "Tennessee Waltz" and "Rocky Top."

b. Almost every state has at least one official state song. Some have more, including Tennessee, which has five, more than any other.

Use It

Read this part of a computer text. Think about how you would sum it up.

If You Need It, Back It Up

If you work on a computer, you must back up your documents. That means to make and save copies of them. Backing up is not difficult or time consuming. Without a backup, you risk losing a document, and that would mean losing all the work that you put into the document. You may be tempted to back up only your most important documents, but a better practice is to back up everything.

Write a summary of "If You Need It, Back It Up."

_____

_____

_____

_____

Putting It in Other Words

♦ *Paraphrasing*

As you read, think about what the writer says and think of other ways to say it. Putting ideas in your own words will help you understand and recall them.

This Is the Idea

Read this part of a history text and put the main idea into other words.

Arthur Wynne's Puzzling Invention

What's a nine-letter word for the puzzle invented by Arthur Wynne in 1913? If you guessed *crossword,* you're almost right. When Wynne's first puzzle appeared in the *New York World,* it was called a word-cross puzzle. He changed the name to *cross-word* a few weeks later.

You could put the main idea of the passage into these other words: "Arthur Wynne created the crossword puzzle in 1913."

Take a Closer Look

Use these steps to put a passage in other words:

- Think about what it means.
- Look away from the text.
- Imagine telling someone what it says.

Read this part of a science text and think about how to put the ideas in other words.

The Capybara

Most rodents, such as mice and rats, are small creatures, but one, the capybara (cap-i-BAR-uh), can weigh more than 100 pounds. Capybaras dwell in and beside shallow inland waters in South America. They eat mainly grasses and leaves. It may sound odd, but people have made capybaras into house pets.

Circle the sentence that puts the ideas in blue ink into other words.

a. Capybaras live along the edges of rivers and lakes in South America and eat plants.

b. Capybaras gather in huge groups throughout the driest regions of desert in South America to eat plants.

Try It

Read this part of a history text and think about how to put
it in other words.

The Travels of Marco Polo — Fact or Fiction?

In the 13th century, Marco Polo journeyed from Italy to
China. At that time, scarcely anyone from European
countries had set foot in that distant land. After years in
China, he returned to Italy and wrote a lengthy account
of his journeys.

Choose one sentence from the article and write it in other words.

_____

_____

Use It

Continue reading the text and think about how to put it in other words.

The account enjoyed wide success. It had a huge influence
on European ideas about China, its people, and its culture. It
is also said that Polo brought Chinese noodles home with
him. That launched Italy's love affair with pasta.

Was Polo's book honest and accurate? Or was it a fake, a way
to build his reputation and line his purse? The likely answer is
that much of what he wrote was based on fact. But he may
have stretched the truth here and there for the sake of his
story. The debate still rages.

Choose one paragraph from the text and write it in other words.

_____

_____

_____

_____

_____

_____

Deciding What It's About

Many signs, charts, and ads are about one topic. Many news reports and articles are about one topic. Sometimes the topic is identified for you. At other times, you have to determine the topic for yourself.

This Is the Idea

Look at this sign and decide what it's about.

Four Easy Ways to Buy a Bus Pass

1 Buy a pass at any station.

2 Buy a pass by phone by calling 555-1234.

3 Buy a pass by mail by calling 555-1234 for a form.

4 Buy a pass online at www.buyyourpass.com.

The words in blue ink help you decide that the topic of this sign is buying a bus pass. The title and the repeated words tell you this. The pictures help you know that you can probably buy your pass by phone, mail, and computer.

Take a Closer Look

Look at these to decide what the topic is:

- titles
- pictures
- headlines or headings
- repeated words on one topic

Look at these ads and decide what each is about.

Buy Bulbs Now!

All bulbs are **on sale** this week, so stock up for your autumn planting season.

Buy Bulbs Now!

All bulbs are on sale this week, so stock up before the dark days of winter arrive.

Write your answers.

1. What is the topic of the ad on the left?

   _____

2. What is the topic of the ad on the right?

   _____

Try It

Look at this part of an instruction sheet and decide what it is about.

Installing on a Wall

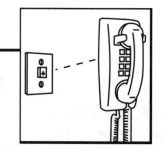

First connect the telephone line cord to the phone jack in the wall. Then line up the pins on the wall plate with the upper portion of the slots in the base plate. Keeping the pins aligned, press the telephone against the wall. Then slide the phone down firmly until it clicks into place.

Write your answers.

1. What is the topic of this paragraph?

_____

2. What other title would be good?

_____

Use It

Look at this part of a history text and decide what it is about.

The Wanderer

In 1931, the cargo ship *Baychimo* became trapped in an ice field off Alaska. A blizzard was coming, and the crew had to go ashore to seek shelter. When the storm was over, they found the ship missing. They assumed it had sunk, but instead it had drifted off alone. For several decades, it was sighted many times, wandering through Arctic waters.

Write your answers.

1. What is the topic of this paragraph?

_____

2. What other title would be good?

_____

Using the Topic

◆ *Anchoring Understanding on the Topic*

This Is the Idea

Which parts of this ad are most important to the topic?

Help Wanted: Driver

Newtown Garden Center wants to hire a part-time driver. Newtown is the oldest garden center in the area. Morning hours mean that parents can be home when school ends. This may be the job you've been waiting for. If you have a clean driving record, call Pam at 555-6789 to apply.

The title tells you that the ad is for a driver. The parts in blue ink are most important to this topic because they tell more about the job and job requirements. The other parts are less important, although they may interest readers.

Take a Closer Look

As you read, ask yourself

- Is this about the topic?
- Is this really important to the topic, or is it something that I don't need to remember?

Which parts of this health brochure are most important to the topic?

Preventing the Spread of Pinkeye

Pinkeye has many causes, and it often spreads quickly, so take steps to prevent its spread. Wash your hands often, and always after handling soiled tissues. Use paper towels instead of cloth when possible, since cloth towels can spread germs that cause pinkeye. Most pinkeye can be treated, so see a doctor soon.

Write two statements that help you to avoid the spread of pinkeye.

1. _____

_____

2. _____

_____

Try It

Which parts of this biography are most important to the topic?

O'Keeffe's Long Career

Georgia O'Keeffe died at the age of 98. She spent more than eight decades of her life as an artist, beginning as a teen when she studied art at home, in Chicago, and in New York. A few years later, she won her first art contest. By age 35, she was famous, and she continued working in the arts until just before she died.

Library of Congress © Carl Van Vechtan
LC-USZ62-116606 DLC

Write your answers.

1. What is the topic?

_____

2. Write two statements that are important to the topic.

_____

_____

Use It

Which parts of this health text are most important to the topic?

Nutritious Snacks

Some snacks, high in sugar or fat, can add to health problems. But other snacks provide needed nutrients. These types of snacks include yogurt, plain fruit or fruit juice, and popcorn without butter. Nuts, dried fruits, or a mixture of the two can also be filling yet nutritious.

Write your answers.

1. What is the topic?

_____

2. Write two statements that are important to the topic.

_____

_____

Finding the Writer's Point

◆ *Recognizing the Main Idea*

Writers sometimes state the point of the writing in a sentence, but sometimes they don't state it. Even if a writer does not state the point, you can often figure it out. It is always a statement about the topic.

This Is the Idea

Read this part of a history text and look for the writer's point.

Glass, the Ancient Modern Material

Today glass often serves as the sleek, gleaming skin of modern skyscrapers, but humans have been making glass for more than 5,000 years. Ancient glass beads and bottles have been found in northern Africa and the Middle East. Early glassmaking was slow and difficult, and glass was as precious as jewels. But the technique of glassblowing, invented about 30 B.C., made glass objects more widely available.

The writer states the main idea up front in the sentence printed in blue ink. The sentences that follow develop the main idea. They give evidence of glassmaking in ancient times.

Take a Closer Look

Read this opinion column and look for the writer's main point.

Enough 10-Best Lists

Am I the only one who is completely fed up with 10-best lists? We've got lists of the 10 best movies, books, songs, television programs, and on and on. I wouldn't be surprised if somebody has listed the 10 best vegetables and the 10 best 10-best lists! I think it's time we stopped this madness.

To find the writer's point

- Look for a general statement about the topic, especially in the first or last sentence.
- Read all the sentences and decide what the writer wants to say about the topic.

Write your answers.

1. What is this column about?

_____

2. What is the writer's point?

_____

Try It

Read this science text and look for the writer's main idea.

The Tide Rises, the Tide Falls

If you've lived near an ocean, you are familiar with tides, the rising and falling of water twice a day. You probably know that the moon's gravity, and to a lesser extent the sun's gravity, causes tides. You may think that lakes and ponds do not have tides. That's a widely held belief, but it's wrong. The moon and sun cause tides in all bodies of water, no matter how large or small they are. But in small bodies of water, the tides are small and difficult to notice.

Getty Images

Write your answers.

1. What is this article about?

   _____

2. What is the writer's main idea?

   _____

   _____

Use It

Read this language text and decide what the main idea is.

Words from Names

The word *sandwich* comes from the Earl of Sandwich, who liked playing cards so much that he wouldn't pause for a meal but put a slice of meat between two slices of bread. The word *saxophone* comes from Sax, the name of its inventor, and apparently the first person to be boycotted was Charles C. Boycott.

Write your answers.

1. What is this article about?

   _____

2. What is the writer's main idea?

   _____

   _____

Using the Writer's Point

◆ *Building on the Main Idea*

First, decide what the writer's point is. (See Lesson 9.) Keep the point in mind as you read. Use it to check your understanding and to help you remember the important parts. Think about other ideas suggested by the point.

This Is the Idea

Read this parenting advice and think about the writer's point.

Getting Beyond "OK"

It's almost a family ritual. On a school-day evening, a parent asks, "How was school?" and the child answers, "OK." Neither the parent nor the child gains anything from the exchange. If you want to find out how your child is doing in school and you want to show that you care, ask specific questions and take the time to listen to specific answers.

The writer's point is that a parent should ask specific questions about the school day. If you are a parent, you might build on that point by thinking about specific questions to ask your child. Then you might think about the kind of answers you hope to get. Then you might put the plan to work.

Take a Closer Look

Read this travel brochure and think about the writer's point.

The Capitol Building

The Capitol building in Washington, D.C., is the center of the government of the United States. The Senate and the House of Representatives have met there for 200 years. Every year, millions of people visit the Capitol. Some visit just for fun, but many want a serious chance to watch government in action.

As you read, ask yourself

- What is important about the writer's point?
- How can I help myself remember the point?
- How can I use the point?

Circle the statement that agrees with the writer's point.

a. The Capitol is most important as a fun place to visit.

b. The Capitol is most important as a government center.

Try It

Read this business text and think about the writer's point.

Your Marketing Plan

If you want to start a business, one of the first steps is to develop a marketing plan. In other words, you have to decide how you are going to persuade people to buy your product or service. Start by thinking about the product or service you will provide. What kind of people are likely to want to buy it?

Circle your answers.

1. Which statement agrees with the writer's point?
   a. A marketing plan is a must for anyone starting a business.
   b. A marketing plan is good, but not really needed.

2. Based on the writer's point, which of the following makes more sense?
   a. open a business and then develop a marketing plan
   b. develop a marketing plan and then open a business

Use It

Read this job-hunting advice and think about the writer's point.

Do Your Homework

Before you go to an interview, find out about the company. Learn about their products or services. Read their ads and any pamphlets or other hand-outs they have. Think about what skills you can offer the company. Discuss the ideas at your interview. You will demonstrate your interest and will likely impress your interviewer.

Write your answers.

1. What is the writer's point?

   _____

   _____

2. The article gives two specific ways to find out about a company. What other way can you think of to find out about a company?

   _____

   _____

Finding Useful Details

◆ *Recognizing Significant Details*

This Is the Idea

Details are the little things in a piece of writing. The most useful details help you understand the main idea. Details that do not help you grasp that idea are not as important.

Which details are useful in getting the main idea of this language text?

How January Got Its Name

The ancient Romans had gods for many everyday things. Pomona was the goddess of trees and fruit. Terminus was the god of boundaries. And Janus was the Roman god of doorways. Stepping through a doorway is one way to begin something new. So, as god of doorways, Janus was also god of new beginnings. **The month that begins our year—January—is named for Janus.**

The main idea is **in bold type.** The sentences in blue ink state important details about this idea. They help you understand why it makes sense for the first month of the year to be named for the Roman god of doorways.

Take a Closer Look

As you read, ask yourself

• Is this detail useful or is it just interesting?

• Does this detail help me understand the writer's main idea?

Which details are useful in deciding whether you can vote?

Who Can Vote?

According to the United States Constitution, any U.S. citizen over the age of 18 can vote in federal elections. However, the states may also add certain requirements that a voter must meet. For example, many states require you to have been living in the state for a certain length of time before you can vote there.

Being 18 is not enough to allow a citizen to vote. What is one detail that shows that? Write your answer.

_____

_____

Try It

Which details help you understand the main idea?

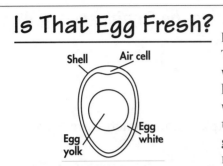

Is That Egg Fresh?

Shell   Air cell

Egg
white

Egg
yolk

Fresh eggs have the best flavor, but older eggs look just as good. To tell whether an unopened egg is fresh, put it in a bowl of water. A fresh egg will sink, but an older egg will stand with the large end up or may even float. Why? A freshly laid egg is filled with liquid, but the contents shrink as it cools. Air seeps through the shell to fill the empty space, forming an air cell. The air cell grows larger as the egg ages, and in time gets big enough to make a "stale" egg float.

List two details that will help you decide whether an egg is fresh.

1. _____

2. _____

Use It

Which details help you understand the main idea?

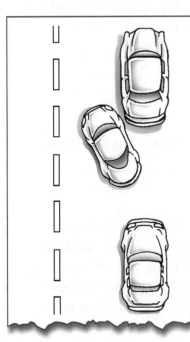

Parallel Parking

Parallel parking: few things are more challenging for a new driver. Even many experienced drivers dread it. But it really isn't hard if you follow the basic steps. First, pull ahead of the empty space. Stop your car so that your rear bumper is lined up with the rear bumper of the car that's parked ahead of the empty space. Keeping your left hand on the steering wheel, turn your upper body so that you can see out the rear window. Slowly back up and slowly turn the steering wheel to the right. You want to get the rear end of your car pointed at a 45° angle toward the center of the empty parking space. When it is pointed that way, turn the steering wheel smoothly to the left as you continue to back up slowly. You will slide right into the space.

List three details that would help you park a car.

1. _____

2. _____

3. _____

Using Details

◆ *Understanding the Significance of Details*

This Is the Idea

Which details in this science text explain how a microwave oven makes food hot?

What Happens in a Microwave Oven

You could say that a microwave oven is a special kind of radio transmitter in a box. The oven makes short radio waves, and those waves vibrate the molecules in the food. When the molecules vibrate and rub together, friction makes the food hot.

The writer says the heat comes from friction when the molecules in the food vibrate and rub together. That detail helps you understand why the food gets hot. Other details tell how the oven makes the molecules vibrate.

Take a Closer Look

Which details help you decide how the ear helps us keep our balance?

Keeping Our Balance

We hear with our ears, of course, but our ears have another function as well. They help us keep our balance. Three small tubes deep inside the ear contain a fluid—a liquid—that moves in the tubes when we move our heads. Tiny cells like little hairs inside the tubes send messages so the brain can tell which way is up even when we're upside down.

The writer doesn't say where the messages from the tiny cells go, but the details help you decide. Where do they go? Write your answer.

As you read, ask yourself

- What makes this detail useful?
- Will this detail help me understand the main idea?
- Will it help me decide what makes sense or fill in other details that are missing?

Try It

Notice details in this part of an employee handbook.

Important Message	
For: _____ Time: _____	
Date: _____	
From: _____	
Phone: _____	
Phoned	Returned your call
Wants to see you	Will call again
Please call	URGENT
Message: _____	
Signed: _____	

Taking Telephone Messages

- Answer the phone, "Worldwide Ventures," and then give your name.
- Ask the caller, "How may I help you?"
- When you take a message, be sure to get the caller's phone number. Check the spelling of the caller's name. Write the message on a message slip.
- Read the message back to the caller to check that it is accurate.

What is one detail that helps you take a message well? Write your answer.

_____

Use It

Look for details that help you guess when people started making tortillas.

Tortillas: The Oldest Bread in America

The process of making corn tortillas is an ancient one that hasn't changed much. You mix corn flour and water to make dough. You roll a bit of dough into a ball and then press the ball into a flat tortilla. You cook the tortilla for about two minutes on a hot pan without fat or oil, turning it so that it cooks evenly on both sides.

This process was invented in Mexico thousands of years ago. Just how long ago isn't known for certain, but scientists think that people began growing corn there about 7,000 years ago.

Getty Images

Do you think the process of making tortillas could be 10,000 years old? What details help you? Write your answer.

_____

_____

_____

Deciding When It Happens

◆ *Following a Sequence*

This Is the Idea

Read this history text. Notice the order of the events.

Fighting Fires in Cities and Towns

Fire control is a special problem in cities and towns because fires spread easily when buildings are close together. The history of fire control in America started in 1631. A damaging fire swept through the small frontier settlement of Boston. As a result, the town passed new fire safety rules for buildings. About 16 years later, New Amsterdam (which later became the city of New York) created the first fire department in the American colonies. Some towns followed New Amsterdam's example, but it was 200 years before most American cities had fire departments.

You can tell that New Amsterdam created a fire department *before* its name was changed to *New York*. The text says the city became New York later.

Take a Closer Look

As you read this science text, notice the order of the steps.

How Caves Form

Caves form in many ways, but one common type is made by water. Water falls as rain and soaks through the soil. When it reaches limestone below the soil, it dissolves the stone. Then, as the water seeps away, it takes the dissolved stone with it. Over time, the water carves an underground room.

What shows the order?
- the order in the text
- dates and times
- key words and phrases, such as *after, as soon as, at last, before, begin, finally, later, next, now, start, then, wait, when,* and *while*

Circle your answers. *Hint:* Which comes before the other in the article?

1. Which of the following steps occurs *before the other?*
   a. Water reaches limestone.   b. Water falls as rain.

2. Which of the following steps occurs *after the other?*
   a. Water dissolves the stone.   b. Rain soaks through soil.

Try It

As you read the following directions, notice the order of the steps.

Taking Better Snapshots

First, compose the photograph. Here is how you do that: Look through the viewfinder and center the photograph on the subject. The subject is the most important part of the picture.

Next, adjust the focus so that the subject is sharp. Then inhale deeply and hold your breath so that you won't jiggle the camera by breathing.

Finally, squeeze the shutter button.

Circle your answers.

1. Which of these steps should you do *second?*
   a. adjust the focus
   b. look through the viewfinder

2. Which of these should you do *just before squeezing the shutter?*
   a. center the photograph
   b. take a breath and hold it

Use It

As you read the following news story, notice the order of the events.

Museum Plans to Expand

NEW CITY — Last week, the New City Museum of Art bought the hotel next door. Today, the museum board announced plans for expansion. Next month, workers will begin tearing the hotel down. After it has been demolished, construction of a new wing will begin. When the new wing is complete, the museum will be three times its present size. The grand reopening is two years away.

Number the following events to show their order.

_____ The hotel has been completely torn down.

_____ The museum board announces plans for expansion.

_____ The new wing is complete.

_____ The museum buys the hotel next door.

_____ The grand reopening takes place.

_____ Construction of the new museum wing begins.

_____ Workers start demolishing the hotel.

Using Time Order

Notice the order of steps or events. Think about why they happen in that order and what would happen if the order were different. Think about what is likely to happen next and what makes sense based on what has happened.

This Is the Idea

Read this article and think about why sequence is important in it.

Rumors

Have you ever played the children's game of telephone? One person whispers a phrase or sentence into the ear of another, who whispers it to a third, and so on, until it has traveled a long way. Then the last person repeats it aloud. The result is invariably wildly distorted from the original. This game shows why rumors are so unreliable. They stray further from the truth each time they are whispered into another ear.

The article is about what happens to a rumor over the course of time. As people pass it on, it becomes distorted and strays further and further from the truth. From what the writer says, you can conclude that to get closer to the truth, you should go back to the original source.

Take a Closer Look

Read this nature text and think about why sequence is important in it.

Tumbleweeds

Most plant species have to spread seeds so the species can thrive. Tumbleweeds do this in a highly unusual way. When a tumbleweed plant is fully grown, its stem weakens until the plant breaks free of its roots. The wind tumbles it along, and it wanders wherever the wind takes it. As it tumbles, seeds fall off, and some of them take root where they fall.

What would happen if the seeds fell off the plant before it began tumbling? Write your answer.

Ask yourself
- Why do the steps or events happen in this order?
- What if the order changed?
- What is likely to happen next?
- What makes sense, based on what has happened?

Try It

Read this instruction sheet and think about the sequence in it.

Auto-Cook Feature

To use the Auto-Cook feature, you must first decide how long the food should cook and when you want it ready.

Press START TIME. Then use the numeric keypad to enter the time when cooking should start.

Press END TIME and enter the time when cooking should stop.

Your meal will be ready when you want it.

Why is it important to begin by deciding how long the food should cook and when you want it ready? Write your answer.

_____

_____

Use It

Read this notice to employees and think about the sequence in it.

To Night Staff:

In the event of a power failure, the water heater will shut down. This is a safety feature designed to ensure that gas will not leak into the building if the electric ignition is not working. The electric ignition lights the water heater's flame.

After a power failure, the water heater must be restarted. (For safety, the system will not let you restart until power has been restored.) To restart, press the red button labeled RESTART and hold it in. Pressing the button starts gas flowing, and holding it in lights the flame. It is very important to hold the button until you are sure that the flame has been lit.

Write your answers. *Hint:* Think about what could happen.

1. Why is it important to hold the button?

_____

_____

2. Why would it be unsafe to restart if the power was still out?

_____

_____

Deciding Why It Happens

◆ *Recognizing Cause and Effect*

Look for causes and effects when you read. To find a cause, ask "Why did this happen?" To find an effect, ask, "What is the result of what happened?" Look for such clues as words, patterns, and pictures.

This Is the Idea

As you read this cooking tip, look for causes and effects.

Removing the Fat

Modern cooks know that a low-fat diet is healthier, so they try to limit the amount of fat in foods. Here is a simple way to remove fat from homemade soup. If you allow the soup to sit for a while, the fat will float to the top. Chilling the soup will make the fat harden and you can remove it easily.

Why are cooks limiting the fat in foods? They know a low-fat diet is healthier. What is the result of allowing soup to sit and then chilling it? The fat floats to the top and hardens, making it easier to remove.

Take a Closer Look

As you read this history text, look for causes and effects.

Root Cellars

Most early houses had nearby root cellars to store fruits and vegetables. The temperature below ground doesn't change much, so the cellars remained cool and moist year round. In cold climates, cellars dug into hillsides were the easiest to reach in winter. Their doors were not buried beneath piles of snow.

Look for

- *because* or *since:* An effect happens because a cause happens.
- *if . . . then:* If a cause happens, then an effect happens.
- *so:* A cause happens, so an effect happens.
- *as a result:* An effect happens as a result of a cause.

Write your answers.

1. Why did root cellars remain cool and moist year round?

_____

2. What was the result of digging cellars into hillsides?

_____

Try It

Think about causes and effects in this paragraph and diagram.

Gears

Gears can transfer movement and change the direction of the movement. Look at the water wheel and axle. The water turns the wheel, so the axle and the gear on it also turn. The teeth on this gear push against the teeth of the next gear, making it turn. However, this gear turns in a new direction.

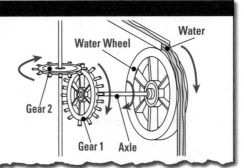

Write your answers.

1. Why does the axle on the water wheel turn?

   _____

2. What results from the first gear pushing against the second gear?

   _____

   _____

Use It

As you read this word history, look for causes and effects.

The Word *Marathon*

We call a long foot race a marathon because of the legendary efforts of one soldier. In 490 B.C., the Greeks defeated the Persians at Marathon, about 26 miles from Athens. This was an important battle, so, the story goes, a soldier ran to Athens to announce the victory. The determined runner never stopped.

Write your answers.

1. Why did the soldier run 26 miles to Athens?

   _____

   _____

2. What resulted from the story of the soldier's race?

   _____

   _____

Using Reasons

◆ *Understanding Cause and Effect*

As you read, look for causes and effects. (See Lesson 15.) Use them to check your understanding, to help you summarize, to predict outcomes, and to make general statements about the text.

This Is the Idea

As you read this home safety tip, look for causes and effects.

Watch Your Back

Your back door may not be protecting you as well as your front door is. Some back doors are sliding doors, which can be lifted from their tracks if they aren't locked in place. Other rear doors have panes of flimsy glass in them. If you replace them with breakproof glass, your door will be more secure.

This paragraph explains that some back doors aren't secure because they might be lifted off their tracks or they might have their glass smashed. It also explains what benefit will result from replacing glass in a door. In general, you can see what changes will result in a more secure door.

Take a Closer Look

As you read, ask yourself

- Why did that happen, or what caused it?
- What resulted from that?

As you read this school note to parents, look for causes and effects.

• *Dress Your Child for Recess*

Children enjoy the exercise of outdoor recess, and they learn better if they have a break. Since recess time is limited, children should have simple outdoor clothing that they can put on quickly. Avoid complicated fasteners and ties.

Write your answers.

1. What is one good effect of a break on schoolchildren?

   _____

2. What might be a bad effect of complicated fasteners and ties?

   _____

Try It

As you read this part of a science text, look for causes and effects.

CATS' NIGHT VISION

Eyes have two types of cells that detect light. The cells called cones see colors well, and the cells called rods detect dim light well. A cat's eye has few cones but many rods, so it sees well in dim light. A cat's eye also contains a special structure called a tapetum. This acts like a mirror, reflecting light back to the rods again. Because the light hits the rods twice, the cat can see even better at night.

Write your answers.

1. What results from the fact that a cat's eye has many rods?

   _____

2. What is likely to result from the fact that a cat's eye has few cones?

   _____

Use It

As you read this cooking information, look for causes and effects.

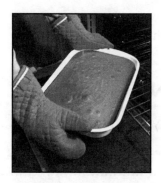

Why Cakes Rise

If you put a little baking soda in a bowl and pour some vinegar on it, the mixture will bubble. The vinegar (an acid) reacts with the baking soda (a base) and releases a gas (the bubbles). This same kind of reaction takes place inside a cake as it bakes. As the bubbles expand, they take up more space and push the batter up. As the batter bakes, it becomes firm, and the bubbles are trapped in place, keeping the cake up.

Write your answers.

1. What results from mixing vinegar and baking soda?

   _____

2. What might result if cake batter does not bake until it's firm?

   _____

Finding Groups

◆ *Recognizing Classification*

Classifying is putting things in groups. Writers usually group things because the things are alike in some way. Notice how the members of a group are alike. Think about other things that might fit in the group.

This Is the Idea

As you read this article for homeowners, notice the groupings in it.

——Driveway Materials——

The basic choice in driveway topping is between loose and solid toppings. Loose toppings include crushed stone and cinders. Solid toppings include asphalt and concrete. Most loose toppings are low in cost but need to be replaced every year or two. Most solid toppings are more costly but last longer.

The writer has put driveway toppings into two groups. Then the writer points out some ways that the toppings in each group are alike. The groups tell you that crushed stone and cinders are likely to be cheaper but less durable than asphalt or concrete.

Take a Closer Look

As you read this catalog contents page, notice how things are grouped.

OUTFITTING THE KITCHEN

Storage: a place for everything and everything in its place ....

Cookware: the right pot for every recipe ....

Glassware: for everything sippable ....

Dishware: from sturdy everyday to special occasion ....

Write your answers.

1. In what section will you find soup bowls for a family dinner?

   _____

2. In what section will you find stainless steel frying pans?

   _____

Try It

Read this chart of license classes and notice how drivers are grouped.

DRIVER'S LICENSE CLASSES			
CLASS A: You may drive any private motor vehicle of less than 8,000 pounds.	**CLASS B:** You may drive any motor vehicle for hire of less than 8,000 pounds.	**CLASS C:** You may drive any single-body motor vehicle of 8,000 pounds or more.	**CLASS E:** You may drive any tractor-trailer combination.

Write your answers.

1. If you want to drive a taxicab, what class of license will you need?

   _____

2. If you want to drive the big trucks that haul goods across the country, what class of license will you need?

   _____

Use It

Read this science text and notice how foods are grouped.

What about the Tomato?

We eat many parts of plants. We may recognize roots like potatoes, bulbs like onions, and leaves like lettuce. We may also recognize flowers like broccoli and stems like celery. But we don't always recognize fruit when we see it. From the point of view of science, a fruit is the part of a flowering plant that contains its seeds. It may be soft, like a grape, or firm, like a string bean, but if it contains the seeds, it is a fruit.

© Corbis Images/PictureQuest

Write your answers.

1. What group does the tomato belong in?

   _____

2. Name some fruits that people usually call "vegetables."

   _____

Using Groups

Writers usually have reasons for making groups. As you read, notice groups and think about why the writer made them. Think about how the groups help you understand the main idea and the general sense of the writing.

This Is the Idea

As you read this part of a news story, notice how people are grouped.

Our Aging City

New predictions suggest that the city's population of children (under 18) is likely to grow by 3 percent over the next 10 years. The adult population (18 to 64) will grow by 6 percent. However, the senior population (65 and older) is likely to grow by as much as 10 percent.

The writer puts people in three groups: children, adults, and seniors. The writer could have given information about smaller groups, such as 9-year-olds. That would have made the general trend harder to see. In general, we can see that older groups are growing faster.

Take a Closer Look

As you read this column, decide why the schools are in groups.

As you read, ask yourself

- Why did the writer put things in groups?
- How are the groups related to the main idea?
- Can I make a general statement about the groups?

School Report Released

The mayor's task force on the city's school buildings has released its report. Of the city's 50 buildings, 25 are in "good" condition. Fifteen are in "fair" condition. Ten buildings are in "poor" condition, bad enough to hinder the educational process. We must start with the poorest and repair them all.

Write your answers.

1. Why are the schools put into groups?

_____

2. What general statement can you make about the groups?

_____

Try It

How do the groups in this table of contents help you make decisions?

Contents ——————————

Chapter 1 — *Something to Start:* Mouthwatering Appetizers ....

Chapter 2 — *Something Hearty:* Hot Soups and Stews ....

Chapter 3 — *Something Light:* Dishes That Don't Add Pounds ....

Chapter 4 — *Something Sweet:* Desserts and Other Treats ....

Write your answers.

1. Why did the writer group the things in Chapter 4?

   _____

2. If you're planning a meal for a cold day, how does grouping help?

   _____

   _____

Use It

How do the groups in this chart help you make decisions?

Attention, Parents: Movie Rating System

G   This movie is OK for all audiences. All ages may come to see it.

PG   Parents should decide whether children may see this movie. Some parts may not be suitable for children.

PG-13   Parents should be careful about letting children under 13 see this movie. Some parts may not be suitable for pre-teens.

R   Children under 17 will not be allowed to see this movie unless a parent or guardian is with them.

NC-17   No one under 17 will be allowed to see this movie.

Write your answers.

1. How does grouping help a parent choose a movie for a child?

   _____

2. What else would a parent consider in choosing a movie for a child?

   _____

   _____

Finding Like and Unlike

◆ *Recognizing Comparison and Contrast*

A writer may compare things, pointing out ways that they are alike. A writer may contrast things, pointing out ways that they are different.

This Is the Idea

As you read this review, notice how the versions are alike and different.

On the Run, the Remake

The classic movie *On the Run* has been remade in living color, rather than the original black and white. The new version has a much faster pace, with more action and exciting special effects. To my surprise, I found that the remake retains the lighthearted humor of the original.

The writer compares and contrasts the two versions of the movie, showing how they are alike *and* different. The pace and the use of color make them different. The humor makes them alike.

Take a Closer Look

As you read this review, notice how the pot pies are alike and different.

Words used to compare

- *also, both, like,* and *same*

Words used to contrast

- *but, however, in contrast, though, while,* and *unlike*
- words that end in *er,* such as *richer*

Pot Pie Taste Test

We tasted chicken pot pies from Yumco and Pieland. The Yumco pie was richer, with a thicker gravy than the Pieland pie. Both pies had about the same amount of chicken, but the Pieland pie had a greater variety of vegetables, while the Yumco pie had only potatoes and carrots.

Write your answers.

1. How are the two chicken pot pies alike?

   _____

2. If a pie contains celery or green beans, which pie is it?

   _____

Try It

Read this chart and decide how the hotels are alike and different.

Hotels in Southern City		KEY	
Empire	🏊 💰	🏊	= swimming pool
Grand	🍽 💰💰💰	🍽	= breakfast
Nova	🏊 🍽 💰💰💰	💰	= budget
State	💰	💰💰💰	= luxury

Write your answers.

1. Which hotel is a good choice for a family of four on a tight budget?

   _____

2. Why might someone choose the Nova over the Grand?

   _____

Use It

Kurt is looking for a used car. He made this chart to help him choose. Read the chart, and notice how the cars are alike and different.

	Options				
	Radio	Shift	AC	Notes	
Lark	yes	auto	yes	low mileage	
Hawk	no	auto	no	looks like new	
Badger	no	std	no	high mileage	
Snark	yes	auto	no	needs some body work	

LARK, '02, auto, air, low miles, great cond. 555-7890.

1. Which car has the most options?

   _____

2. How are the Hawk and Snark alike?

   _____

3. What is one way that the Lark and Badger are different?

   _____

Using What You Find

◆ *Understanding Comparison and Contrast*

Look for statements that compare and contrast things. (See Lesson 19.) Use what you find to get a general idea about the things. Use it to make choices. Use it to fill gaps in the writing.

This Is the Idea

Why are likenesses and differences important in this chart?

CHOOSING INTERNET ACCESS	
Telephone Dial-Up	**Cable Connection**
• limited connection time	• always connected
• slower downloads	• faster downloads
• no installation fee	• installation fee

The chart shows differences between two types of Internet access. These differences are important if you want to get Internet access or change the type. However, the chart doesn't tell what each type costs; you would have to check.

Take a Closer Look

Why are differences important in this product review?

Think about

- what makes things alike or different
- what you can say in general about the likenesses and differences
- why the likenesses and differences are important
- what they suggest that isn't said

TWO "STARTER" BICYCLES FOR CHILDREN

Both of these bikes are designed to give the youngest riders a taste of two-wheel fun. The Whizzer has small "training" wheels at the back that stabilize the bike but can be removed to make it a true two-wheeler. The Doubler is really a tricycle, but the wheels are large, and the two at the rear are close together. This gives it a bicycle "look" and a more stable ride than the Whizzer has.

Write your answers.

1. Which bike is more likely to be wobbly and unsteady?

   _____

2. Which bike can be adjusted for an older child?

   _____

Try It

This product guide compares heating systems. Think about differences.

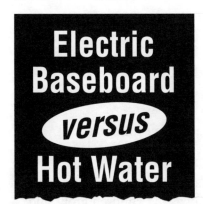

Electric baseboard heat costs little to install and is quiet, but it may make household air too dry. It turns on and off quickly as temperatures change. Hot-water heat requires plumbing and may be costly to install. It gives a gentle, even heat because the water is not much hotter than the air. For the same reason, however, it may react slowly to temperature changes.

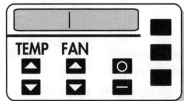

Which differences are most important when choosing a type of heat? Why? Write your answer.

_____

_____

Use It

Read this chart, which compares common investments.

TYPE	HOW IT CAN MAKE MONEY	RISK
U.S. savings bonds	You lend money to the U.S. government. It pays you back with interest over time. Returns are low to moderate.	none
Bonds	You lend money to a company or government. It pays you back with interest over time. Returns vary.	low to moderate
Mutual fund	You buy a share in an investment fund. If it has profits, it pays you. If the value goes up, you can sell for a profit. Returns vary.	low to high
Stocks	You buy a share in a company. If the value goes up, you can sell for a profit. If the company makes money, it may pay you something. Returns vary.	low to high

If you were choosing an investment, what factors would you think about? Why? Write your answer.

_____

_____

Guessing What Will Happen

As you read, think about what is likely to happen as time passes. Predict what will happen. Use what you know and any hints that the writer gives you.

This Is the Idea

Read this advice and predict what will happen if you follow it.

KEEPING TRACK OF PROGRESS

Many parents mark children's height on the edge of a doorway as the children grow, and children delight in seeing the marks march upward. You can't mark a child's progress in thinking and learning on a doorway, but there is another way. Save a selection of the child's school papers, in order, in a binder, and look at them together now and then.

From the statement in blue ink, you can predict that a child will also be delighted to see progress in schoolwork. The writer suggests that the child will say, in effect, "Look how much I've grown in thinking and learning."

Take a Closer Look

Read this science text and make predictions.

These help you guess what will happen

- a pattern of events
- the writer's point and conclusions
- causes and effects
- what you know and your own good guesses

Sleeping Seeds

Plants that reproduce from seeds generally release seeds once a year. This can sometimes put the seeds in danger. The plant might release seeds during a drought, for example. However, seeds have the ability to remain *dormant*, to "sleep." Instead of sprouting during a drought, the seed waits until conditions change for the better.

What do you predict is likely to happen if a seed sprouts during a drought? Write your answer.

_____

_____

Try It

Read this small-business advice and make predictions.

The Mystery of Shrinkage

Suppose that you have a small business baking and selling cookies. You add up all your costs, including ingredients, packaging, gas, and electricity, and set your prices to give yourself a nice profit. Wait a minute. You forgot to allow for what businesses call "shrinkage" —what is lost to waste, breakage, or sampling.

Write your answers.

1. If you don't allow for shrinkage, will your costs be lower or higher than you expect?

_____

2. If you don't allow for shrinkage, will your profits be lower or higher than you expect?

_____

Use It

Read this news article and make predictions.

Drought Worsens

SOUTHERN CITY — The city is in the grip of the worst drought in years. Water levels in area reservoirs are far below normal. "We are at a decision point," said the mayor, "and I have drafted water-saving regulations in case we need them." Forecasters say that no rain is in store for at least a week. The last time drought conditions were this severe, the city banned all watering of lawns and closed all swimming pools.

How do you predict life in Southern City will change if the drought lasts much longer? Write your answer.

_____

_____

Using Your Prediction

◆ *Applying Predictions of Outcome*

A prediction is a good guess about what may happen as time passes. (See Lesson 21.) Use a prediction to check your understanding and to plan what you should do. Use it to test what the writer says, including opinions, and to test general statements.

This Is the Idea

Read this energy-saving tip. Think about what you should do.

> ### The Easiest Energy Tip of All
>
> Look around your home to see whether your heating or cooling vents are blocked. You'd be amazed how many people push sofas, shelves, or wardrobes against these outlets. Others lay rugs over vents. If any of the vents are blocked, the heating or cooling system has to work longer and harder.

You read the advice and think about what may happen in different cases. You predict that if you move things away from vents, the heating or cooling system will achieve its result with less work. From that, you predict that you will save energy and may be more comfortable.

Take a Closer Look

Read these directions and think about what you should do to get a rebate.

> ## TO GET YOUR REBATE
>
> Thank you for buying the Whisper Fan! To take advantage of our rebate offer, you must mail in your store receipt and the serial number label from the product package. Copies are not acceptable. Mail before August 31 to the address below.

What will happen if you send a photocopy of your store receipt instead of the original? Write your answer.

You may want to

- stop something from happening
- make sure that something does happen
- check your understanding
- test an opinion
- check a general statement

Try It

Read this advice and think about what will happen when you brake.

You and Your Bicycle Brakes

When you're getting your bicycle ready for spring, pay attention to the brakes. Take a test ride in a safe area and try stopping. If you have to squeeze the brake levers all the way down or don't stop smoothly, your brakes need adjusting. If the pads are badly worn, they must be replaced. When you're riding, applying the rear brake more strongly than the front one will help you steer a straight line. If you're riding in the rain, remember that the brake pads may slip when you brake.

Write your answers.

1. What is likely to happen if you apply the front brake more strongly than the rear brake?

   _____

2. What is likely to happen if the pads slip when you brake in the rain?

   _____

Use It

Read this opinion column and predict what drowsy drivers may do.

Drowsy? Don't Drive

People who drive when they are overtired put themselves and others at risk. Their vision is blurred, their reaction time is slow, and their judgment is fuzzy. A drowsy driver is nearly as dangerous behind the wheel as a drunk driver. Take my advice: if you're drowsy, stop the car and sleep it off.

Write your answers.

1. What can you predict about how you will drive when you are drowsy?

   _____

2. Based on your prediction, what do you think of the writer's advice?

   _____

Thinking Clearly

◆ *Drawing Conclusions*

Statements often work together. They may be linked by grouping, by cause and effect, or by likenesses and differences. When you read one statement that makes sense, you may be able to conclude, or figure out, another statement that makes sense.

This Is the Idea

What can you conclude about free tickets from this history text?

Annie Oakley and "Annie Oakleys"

Annie Oakley was a sharpshooter in Buffalo Bill's Wild West Show. She threw a playing card into the air and shot holes through it. Later, when show producers gave out free tickets punched with holes, people called them "Annie Oakleys" because they looked like cards after she had shot them.

The article tells about a cause and an effect. The cause was Annie Oakley's shooting holes in playing cards. The effect was people's calling punched tickets Annie Oakleys. You can conclude that if producers had marked free tickets with an *X* instead of punching them, people wouldn't have called them Annie Oakleys.

Remember

- What is true for a group is true for each member.
- If X is bigger than Y, then Y is smaller than X.
- If something happens, there must be a reason.

Take a Closer Look

What can you conclude about "wheelers" from this announcement?

HOSPITAL SEEKS VOLUNTEERS

Moss Memorial Hospital seeks volunteers to work evenings and weekends. Some jobs involve working with patients; others do not. You might enjoy working in the gift shop, at the front desk, or in one of the labs. We also need lots of "wheelers" to wheel patients to appointments in the hospital.

Circle the statement that describes what you can conclude. ***Hint:*** What is true for a group is true for each member.

a. If you were a "wheeler," you would not be a volunteer.
b. If you were a "wheeler," you would help patients directly.
c. If you were a "wheeler," you would work in the gift shop.

Try It

What can you conclude about how to use this memory tip?

Remembering Lists

The Great Lakes

At times, you may need to memorize a list of objects or names. One common way is to take the first letter of each item in the list and make a single word out of these letters. For example, many people use the word *HOMES* to remember the names of the five Great Lakes.

Write your answers.

1. What can you conclude about the names of the Great Lakes?

2. Suppose you want to get ingredients for a fruit salad. You need strawberries, raspberries, apples, and tangerines. What word might help you remember the list?

Use It

What can you conclude about refinancing from this bank ad?

Should You Refinance?

Should you get a new mortgage if interest rates drop? Decide for yourself. First, add up all the costs of getting the new mortgage. The fees can total thousands of dollars. Then compare these costs with the annual savings you expect from the lower rate. How long will it be before your savings are greater than the costs? Do you plan to stay in your home that long?

Write your answers.

1. A couple follows the directions in the ad. They find that their savings will be greater than the costs after four years. They plan to stay in their home for two more years. Would refinancing be a good idea?

2. Would refinancing be a good idea if they plan to stay for 10 years?

Using Clear Thinking

Decide what you can conclude from what you read. (See Lesson 23.) Use what you conclude to check your understanding, to decide what you should do, or to judge an opinion.

This Is the Idea

What can you conclude about this medical advice?

KEEP YOUR GUMS HEALTHY

You should see a dentist regularly for the sake of your gums. Gum disease is the primary reason for tooth loss in adults. Since gum disease is often painless, many people don't even realize that they have it. By the time they notice any problem, the disease may be quite advanced.

The writer states an opinion in the first sentence. When you read further, you learn that gum disease causes tooth loss. From the last two sentences, you can conclude that you might have gum disease and not know it. You can use this conclusion to judge the writer's opinion.

Take a Closer Look

What can you conclude from this column about cutting tree branches?

Think safety first when you remove large tree branches. Power saws can slip, especially if you do not have firm footing. Never use one while standing on a ladder. Even the best ladders can be shaky, and a small slip can cause a serious injury. And remember that tree limbs are heavy and can do damage if they fall in the wrong place. To prevent problems, hire a tree service to cut large branches close to homes or power lines.

Write your answers.

1. What is one thing that could go wrong when cutting branches with a power saw?

   _____

2. What can you conclude about what a tree service can do?

   _____

Try It

What can you conclude about buying a used car?

Buying a Used Car

A car is a major purchase, so consider more than the looks before you decide to buy. Inspect it well, or pay someone else to check it for you. No used car is perfect, but you want to avoid serious flaws that will be costly to fix. A trained mechanic can find them if you can't.

Write your answers.

1. What do a used car's looks tell you about how well it will run?

_____

2. Who should pay a mechanic to check a used car?

_____

Use It

What can you conclude about compound interest from this financial article?

COMPOUND INTEREST

Most banks pay compound interest on savings accounts. Suppose you have $1,000 in an account that pays 1% annual interest, compounded monthly. Every month, the bank calculates 1% of your balance, takes one-twelfth of the amount (for one month out of the year), and adds it to your balance. Your balance would change as shown in the table to the right.

Month	Starting Balance	Interest	Ending Balance
1	$1,000.00	$.83	$1,000.83
2	$1,000.83	$.83	$1,001.66
3	$1,001.66	$.83	$1,002.49
4	$1,002.49	$.84	$1,003.33
5	$1,003.33	$.84	$1,004.17
6	$1,004.17	$.84	$1,005.01

Write your answers.

1. In the example given, what will the starting balance be in month 7?

_____

2. If you leave the money in the bank, how will the balance change in future months?

_____

Filling Gaps

◆ *Making Inferences*

This Is the Idea

Read this part of a sports column and think about the writer's main idea.

Like Night and Day

The baseball season is half over, and it's time to say that the Gold Sox have a real chance to win the pennant this year. There is a new sense of pride and confidence among the players. When you watch them take the field, you feel that they have put the past behind them. They're good this year, very good, and they know it.

As you read, you learn that the Gold Sox are good this year, but you can guess something else. You can guess that the Sox haven't been very good in the past, and that they didn't have much pride or confidence. Without saying so directly, the writer is comparing the old Sox and the new Sox.

Take a Closer Look

What do the details in this travel tip suggest about Westville?

A visit to Westville is delightful at any time of year, but we think summer is best because we love the salt air and gentle breezes, the cry of the gulls, prowling the quaint shops along scenic Front Street, and strolling along the boardwalk. A visit to the Westville lighthouse is always a must, as is at least one moonlit clambake.

As you read, ask yourself

- Can I connect ideas to come up with new ones?
- Do my new ideas make sense, based on what I read?

Circle the answer that is a good guess about Westville. *Hint:* Think about how the details add up.

a. It's a large inland city in the Southwest.

b. It's a small seacoast town.

Try It

Read this science text and think about prairie dogs' habits.

PRAIRIE DOGS

Prairie dogs are rodents, like squirrels and mice. They live in groups called towns and dig long burrows or tunnels. During the warmer months, they retreat to their burrows during the hottest part of the day. In the winter, they may stay underground for several days in especially cold weather. But they emerge to bask on sunny afternoons.

© Photo 24/Brand X Pictures/ PictureQuest

Write your answers.

1. Why do prairie dogs stay in the burrow during the summer months?

_____

2. Why do prairie dogs stay in the burrow during the winter months?

_____

Use It

Read this science text and think about the two locations.

Getty Images

The Arctic and the Antarctic are at opposite ends of the Earth, and both have begun to interest tourists. Touring the Arctic is possible, although visiting the North Pole is not yet a casual trip. Tourists in the Arctic can expect to see polar bears, walruses, and whales. Touring the Antarctic is still largely a dream. Would-be tourists shudder at the thought of the climate, and rules intended to preserve Antarctica's natural state discourage casual trips. Antarctica has no land mammals at all. However, it is home to the penguin.

Write your answers.

1. Is the Antarctic in the north or the south?

_____

2. What can you infer about the climate of the Antarctic?

_____

Using Good Guesses

◆ *Applying Inferences*

An inference is a good guess about something that the writer suggests but does not say. (See Lesson 25.) Use inferences to learn more about a topic and to decide whether the writer's statements make sense.

This Is the Idea

Read this health tip and think about the writer's opinion.

Fashion or Feet

It's foolish to choose shoes for the sake of fashion rather than the sake of your feet. Are you tempted by shoes with soaring high heels and tapered toes? Ask yourself whether you're willing to pay for them with chronic heel pain later in life or with permanently deformed toes.

The writer states a strong opinion in the first sentence. The rest of the paragraph suggests the writer's reasons for that opinion, but doesn't state them directly. You can infer that high heels can cause chronic heel pain and tapered toes can deform toes. You can also infer that avoiding high heels and tapered toes would be good for your feet.

Take a Closer Look

Read this part of a history text and think about the writer's topic.

There is probably one near you now, in the corner of a few papers, holding them together. That gadget was invented by Thomas Briggs about a hundred years ago. The first machine for poking metal legs through paper and bending them over to make them hold tight was huge. Briggs took that idea and adapted it so the machine would fit on a desk.

As you read, ask yourself

- Do some ideas suggest other ideas?
- Can I use those new ideas to extend what the writer says?

Circle your answers.

1. Which of these is a good guess about the writer's topic?
   a. the paper clip
   b. the staple

2. Which of these is a good guess about Briggs?
   a. He invented the desktop machine and the large version.
   b. He invented the desktop machine but not the large version.

Try It

Read this beginning of an article and think about the writer's opinions.

A Bit of Wisdom

A wise guide once told a group of mountain climbers, "Getting to the top is optional, but getting down is not." Many people make the mistake of focusing on one big event, like getting out of school, having a child, or retiring. They don't plan what they will do after the event is over and they have to "get down."

Write your answers.

1. Would you infer that the rest of this article will be about ways to get down a mountain or ways to plan for life?

   _____

2. Would you infer that the writer agrees with the guide?

   _____

Use It

Read this beginning of a science text and think about the writer's point.

"SEEING" WITH EARS

Although many people think that bats are blind, they are not. However, bats do not see well at night, and that's a problem because they hunt for food at night. The bats' solution to this problem is to use the ears to aid the eyes. The bat makes high-pitched sounds and listens for the echoes. The echoes allow bats to find the insects they eat and avoid obstacles.

© PhotoLink/PhotoDisc/PictureQuest

Write your answers.

1. What can you infer about how well bats hear?

   _____

2. What can you infer about echoes from insects and echoes from walls or trees?

   _____

   _____

Getting the Big Picture

◆ *Making Generalizations*

As you read, pause now and then to step back from the details. Think about the general meaning of the text. If you can, make a general statement based on the details.

This Is the Idea

What can you say in general about this news report?

Mayor Announces More Budget Cuts

SOUTHERN CITY — The mayor's office announced cuts in the school budget today, just two days after the announcement of cuts in the police department budget. Last week, cuts in the budgets for the city's library system and fire department were announced.

In general, you could say that the mayor has made many cuts in the city budget. You might also say that the mayor thinks that the city should cut its spending.

Take a Closer Look

As you read, ask yourself
- What is the general idea?
- If the writer doesn't state one, can I make a good guess at one?

What can you say in general about the trend shown on this graph?

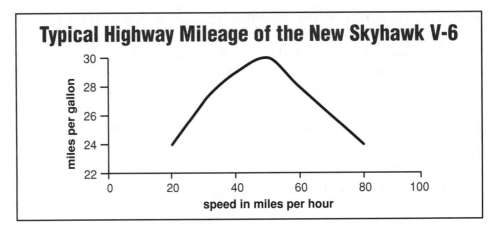

Typical Highway Mileage of the New Skyhawk V-6

Based on the graph, circle the better general statement about the Skyhawk V-6.

a. Gas mileage goes down as speed increases.
b. The engine is most efficient at around 50 miles per hour.

Try It

What can you say in general about the trends shown on this graph?

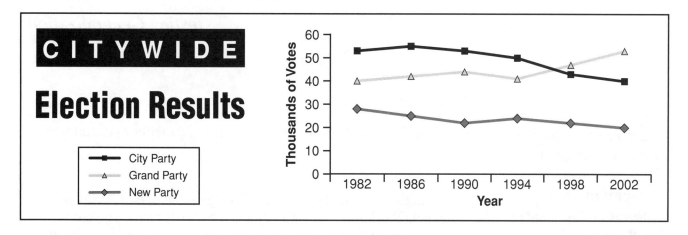

Write your answers.

1. Which party or parties became more popular in the last 20 years?

   _____

2. In the next election, which party do you predict will come in last?

   _____

Use It

Based on this article, what can you say about potatoes in general?

The Humble (or Noble) Potato

They are eaten baked, boiled, fried, mashed, stuffed, whipped, and chipped. There are kinds called fingerling, butterball, Yukon gold, and red bliss. Some are round and fat, others long and thin. Some have white flesh, others yellow, red, and even purple. They are filling and rich in vitamin C, and yet a medium-size potato has only about 100 calories and virtually no fat before you fry it or add butter.

Write your answers and your reasons.

1. Are potatoes a good choice for people who enjoy variety in food?

   _____

2. Are potatoes a good choice for people interested in healthy eating?

   _____

Checking the Big Picture

◆ *Testing Generalizations*

As you read, pause now and then to make a general statement about the facts and ideas in the text. (See Lesson 27.) Look for general statements that the writer makes, too. Decide whether they fit the facts.

This Is the Idea

Think about the general statement in this part of a letter to the editor.

> *To the Editor:*
>
> Last night I attended one of the City League baseball games in my neighborhood, and I was shocked by what I saw. The coach on one team treated his young players horribly, shouting at them when they made the smallest error. The coaches in this league are out of control.

The writer makes a general statement about the coaches in the City League. However, that general statement is based on what the writer saw one coach do at one game. The writer hasn't given enough information to support a general statement.

Take a Closer Look

As you read, ask yourself

- Does the writer have enough information to make a general statement?
- Does the general statement fit the facts and cover all the facts without going too far?
- Is the statement fair?

Think about the general statement in this product review.

> **The Mammoth X10 Pickup**
>
> Mammoth Motors advertises the X10 as "the truck that can take it," so we drove an X10 from Los Angeles to New York to find out how well the truck can take it. Our X10 developed an annoying rattle by the time we reached Nevada, and the air conditioner stopped working in Missouri. Mammoth should start calling the X10 "the truck that can't take it."

Write your answers.

1. How many X10 trucks did the writer test?

   _____

2. Does the writer have enough information?

   _____

3. Is the general statement fair?

   _____

Try It

Think about the writer's general statements in this column.

Not-So-Rapid Transit

Our city's transit system is slow and unreliable. After waiting more than half an hour in the rain for a bus last week, I decided to check buses against the published schedule. Buses on the C1 route in my neighborhood were behind schedule more than 60 percent of the time. Buses on other routes are probably just as bad, and quite possibly much worse.

Write your answers.

1. The writer says that "Our city's transit system is slow and unreliable." What is wrong with that general statement?

   _____

2. What would be a better general statement?

   _____

Use It

Think about the writer's general statements in this letter.

Dear Hana,

I'm enjoying my visit to this amazing city, but I have to say that the people here are very rude. I stopped on the sidewalk to take some pictures of the skyscrapers. People rushing on their way to work kept bumping into me. No one even said "sorry." When I got onto a bus and asked for change, the driver didn't even answer me. He just pointed to a sign that said, "Exact change only."

Write your answers.

1. The writer says that "the people here are very rude." What is wrong with that general statement?

   _____

2. What would be a better general statement?

   _____

Finding the Facts

◆ *Separating Fact from Opinion*

A fact is true and can be proved, but an opinion cannot be proved. An opinion is what someone feels or believes. Different people may have different opinions about the same topic, but facts are true for everyone.

This Is the Idea

Which parts of this explanation are statements of fact?

Getting around the Internet

The Internet and World Wide Web are great inventions, and Web browsers make them a joy to use. A browser is software that can look up an Internet address. If you type www.place.com into a browser, that tells the software where to look. It works like a postal address, since every machine on the Internet has a unique address.

The statements in blue ink are facts that you could prove. You could find articles about the Internet that would tell you about browsers. You can't prove that the Internet and Web are great inventions or that Web browsers make them a joy to use. Those are opinions.

Take a Closer Look

Which parts of this notice are statements of fact?

To spot facts

- Look for statements that you can check.

To spot opinions

- Look for words such as *should* or *must*.
- Look for suggestions that something is good or bad.

For Your Safety at Sea

This ship carries inflatable life rafts instead of lifeboats. These new rafts will amaze you. They have covers that keep out waves and provide shelter. They contain food, water, fishing gear, and flares. They even send radio signals for a week. Every ship should have enough of them for all aboard.

1. Write one fact from "For Your Safety at Sea."

_____

2. Write one opinion from "For Your Safety at Sea."

_____

Try It

Which parts of this sign are opinions?

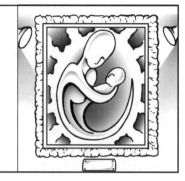

Mother's Day Exhibit

Mother's Day is one of America's favorite holidays.
This Mother's Day, Brandt Gallery will have an exhibit
of portraits of famous mothers. The show will begin with
a brunch at 11:00 A.M. All of the artists will attend.
This show is a perfect way to celebrate the day with your mother.

Write one opinion from this sign.

_____

_____

Use It

Which parts of this sports history are facts? Which are opinions?

Changes in Golf Equipment

The first golf balls can't have been much fun to use.
They were smooth on the outside and stuffed with
feathers. Later, golf balls were made of hard rubber.
These flew farther than the older ones. Golf balls
became more exciting in the early 1900s. Dimples on
the surface changed the air pattern around the balls.
This let them fly faster and higher than earlier ones.

Today, there are two kinds of golf balls. One kind—
wound balls—have a core surrounded by a tightly
wound rubber thread. Because of the way they spin, these balls
give skilled golfers more control. But you should avoid using them
if you're not very good. Less-skilled golfers tend to do better with
two-piece balls, which have no rubber thread.

Write one fact and one opinion from this sports history.

Fact: _____

_____

Opinion: _____

_____

Checking the Facts

◆ Evaluating Statements of Fact

You can check facts in a dictionary, encyclopedia, atlas, or almanac. (The famous *Farmer's Almanac* isn't good for checking facts. A statement might sound like a fact but really may be a joke or a folktale.)

This Is the Idea

Read this part of an article and decide where you could check the facts.

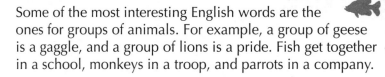

ANIMALS IN GROUPS

Some of the most interesting English words are the ones for groups of animals. For example, a group of geese is a gaggle, and a group of lions is a pride. Fish get together in a school, monkeys in a troop, and parrots in a company.

The article is about the words used in English to name groups of animals. You could check the facts in a dictionary or an encyclopedia. If you have access to the Internet, you could search for the terms and try to find Web pages about them. An atlas or almanac wouldn't help you.

Take a Closer Look

Read this geography text and decide where you could check the facts.

New Zealand

New Zealand

Because it is an island nation, New Zealand has an unusual animal population. Until people arrived on New Zealand, there were no land mammals there, though there were bats, which are flying mammals. There were no snakes at all, either, and there are none today. However, New Zealand has an enormous variety of birds.

Use these sources to check facts:

- A dictionary gives facts about words.
- An encyclopedia gives facts about general subjects.
- An atlas gives facts about countries of the world.
- An almanac gives facts about events of the past year.

Write your answers.

1. Where could you check to see if New Zealand is an island nation?

   _____

2. Would an almanac help you check the statement about bats?

   _____

Try It

Read this part of an article and decide where you could check the facts.

The Sloth

The sloth (pronounced *slawth*) is an animal that lives in the forests of South and Central America. Sloths spend their entire lives hanging upside down from the limbs of trees. The trees provide them with their food, primarily leaves, and keep them out of the reach of other animals. Sloths are nocturnal, sleeping all day and becoming active at night.

Write your answers.

1. Where could you check the pronunciation of *sloth?*

    _____

2. Where could you check the statement about sleeping all day?

    _____

Use It

Read this part of an article and decide where you could check the facts.

Global Warming

Many scientists say that "greenhouse gases" are causing a gradual warming of the global climate. These gases are released when oil and gas are burned to heat homes or power cars. Some other scientists argue that we do not have enough information to show that humans are changing the world's climate. They point out that the world's weather and temperatures vary greatly over time and from place to place.

Write your answers.

1. Where could you check whether "greenhouse gases" come from burning oil and gas?

    _____

2. Where could you look to find scientists' latest ideas about global warming?

    _____

Thinking About Opinions

An opinion is what someone feels or believes. Look for reasons and facts when you judge an opinion. Reasonable opinions are backed up by facts, research, and good reasons.

This Is the Idea

Look for facts and opinions in this article from a local paper.

TellCell Tower Talks

On Monday night, the Zoning Board plans a hearing on the proposed TellCell phone tower. TellCell wants to build a cell phone tower on Pitt's Hill. Many voters have voiced concerns about this. More than 200 have said that they plan to attend. This meeting is likely to be heated and controversial.

The writer gives facts in every sentence but the last. The last states the opinion that the meeting will be heated and controversial. Could you predict that after reading the facts? Voters are concerned about this issue, so it's reasonable to think that they will discuss it with some passion.

Take a Closer Look

When you read opinions, ask

- Does the writer support the opinions with facts, research, and reasons?
- Could I have predicted the opinion from the facts?

Read this part of a letter. Think about the writer's opinion.

Give Your Support

Almost 60 million people in this country now use cell phones. They use them for business, for safety, and to keep in touch. Phones don't work well in places without towers. The group that wants to block this tower has nothing but their own interests at heart. They must be stopped.

Write your answers.

1. What does the writer think about the cell phone tower?

   _____

2. What is one reason or fact that the writer gives?

   _____

Try It

Read this part of a letter, and think about the writer's opinion.

Not So Fast

Cell phone towers look ugly even when they are disguised as trees. They also transmit radio waves, which some people think have a negative effect on health. No one knows what happens at low levels over a long time. Scientists are still studying the health risk of cell towers, so we should wait to build one.

Write your answers.

1. What is the writer's opinion about building a cell phone tower?

   _____

2. What is one fact that the writer gives to support this opinion?

   _____

Use It

Read this part of a letter. Based on the reasons and facts, predict the writer's opinion.

Impact on Wildlife

Each year, more than four million birds are killed by cell phone towers. Many of these birds are songbirds, which fly at night. On cloudy nights, the birds fly lower than usual. The lights or the radio waves from the towers attract them. Then the birds fly into the guy wires and are killed.

Getty Images

Circle your answer.

1. Which opinion do you predict this writer would hold?
   a. The tower should be built as soon as possible.
   b. Some alternative to the tower should be found.

Write your answer.

2. What is one reason or fact that supports that opinion?

   _____

   _____

Answer Key

Lesson 1

Take a Closer Look

1. exploring caves
2. a spelunker without training and experience

Try It

1. a long, winding ridge of gravel and sand
2. water flowing from a melting glacier
3. a heap of sand, soil, and rock left behind as a glacier retreated

Use It

1. bend
2. twinkling
3. misleading; likely to fool someone

Lesson 2

Take a Closer Look

1. a   2. b

Try It

1. quickly
2. slowly

Use It

1. Answers will vary.
2. Read the article slowly and carefully to get the details.

Lesson 3

Take a Closer Look

1. Answers will vary.
2. parents or others who care for children

Try It

1. the moon's
2. The Earth passes between the sun and the moon, and its shadow falls on the moon.

Use It

1. a device like a zipper
2. He wanted a quicker and easier way to fasten boots.

3. A slide slipped the hooks into the eyes.

Lesson 4

Take a Closer Look

1. should be put under What I Know
2. should be put under What I Want to Know

Try It

Answers will vary, but should be put under What I Learned.

Use It

Answers will vary.

Lesson 5

Take a Closer Look

a, b

Try It

b

Use It

Answers will vary.

Lesson 6

Take a Closer Look

a

Try It

Answers will vary.

Use It

Answers will vary.

Lesson 7

Take a Closer Look

1. flower bulbs to plant
2. light bulbs

Try It

1. installing a phone on a wall
2. Answers will vary.

Use It

1. a cargo ship that drifted, or wandered, through Arctic waters
2. Answers will vary.

Lesson 8

Take a Closer Look

1. Wash your hands often and always after handling soiled tissues.
2. Use paper towels instead of cloth when possible, since cloth towels can spread germs that cause pinkeye.

Try It

1. Georgia O'Keeffe's long career as an artist
2. Answers will vary.

Use It

1. healthy snacks
2. Answers will vary.

Lesson 9

Take a Closer Look

1. 10-best lists
2. We should stop making 10-best lists.

Try It

1. tides
2. The moon and sun cause tides in all bodies of water.

Use It

1. words that come from people's names
2. Some words come from the names of people.

Lesson 10

Take a Closer Look

b

Try It

1. a   2. b

Use It

1. Before you go to an interview, find out about the company.
2. Answers will vary.

Lesson 11

Take a Closer Look

Many states require you to have been living in the state for a certain length of time before you can vote there.

Try It

1. A fresh egg will sink.
2. An older egg will stand with the large end up or may even float.

Use It

Answers will vary.

Lesson 12

Take a Closer Look

to the brain

Try It

Answers will vary.

Use It

No, it's probably not more than 7,000 years old. Tortillas were invented in Mexico, and scientists think people started growing corn there 7,000 years ago.

Lesson 13

Take a Closer Look

1. b   2. a

Try It

1. a   2. b

Use It

4, 2, 6, 1, 7, 5, 3

Lesson 14

Take a Closer Look

The seed wouldn't be spread.

Try It

because that allows you to decide when cooking should start and stop

Use It

1. If you didn't hold the button, you would start the gas flowing without lighting it.

2. If you turned on the gas, there would be no power to light the flame.

Lesson 15

Take a Closer Look

1. because the temperature below ground doesn't change much

2. In cold climates, the cellars were easier to reach in winter because the doors weren't buried under piles of snow.

Try It

1. because the water turns the wheel

2. The second gear turns, but in a different direction from the first.

Use It

1. to announce that the Greeks had defeated the Persians

2. The word *marathon* came to mean a long foot race.

Lesson 16

Take a Closer Look

1. Answers will vary.

2. The clothes take too long to put on.

Try It

1. It sees well in dim light.

2. It doesn't see colors well.

Use It

1. The mixture releases a gas.

2. The bubbles won't be trapped in place, and the cake will fall.

Lesson 17

Take a Closer Look

1. Dishware

2. Cookware

Try It

1. Class B

2. Class E

Use It

1. fruit

2. Answers will vary. Possible answers include green peppers, cucumbers, squash, and pumpkins.

Lesson 18

Take a Closer Look

1. to show how much repair work the school buildings need

2. Answers will vary.

Try It

1. so that a person could find all the sweets in one place

2. All the hearty dishes are in one chapter. You don't have to look through the whole book for them.

Use It

1. It matches suitable movies to age groups of children.

2. Answers will vary.

Lesson 19

Take a Closer Look

1. They have the same amount of chicken.

2. the Pieland pie

Try It

1. the Empire

2. They cost about the same, but the Nova has a pool and the Grand doesn't.

Use It

1. the Lark

2. They have automatic transmissions and don't have air conditioning.

3. Answers will vary.

Lesson 20

Take a Closer Look

1. the Whizzer

2. the Whizzer

Try It

Answers will vary.

Use It

Answers will vary.

Lesson 21

Take a Closer Look

The young plant would not grow well and might die.

Try It

1. The costs will be higher.
2. The profits will be lower.

Use It

Answers will vary.

Lesson 22

Take a Closer Look

You won't get the rebate.

Try It

1. It will be harder to steer in a straight line.
2. It will take more time and distance to stop.

Use It

1. You will drive poorly.
2. Answers will vary.

Lesson 23

Take a Closer Look

b

Try It

1. They begin with the letters *H, O, M, E,* and *S.*
2. Answers will vary. Possible answers: ARTS, RATS, STAR, TARS.

Use It

1. no
2. yes

Lesson 24

Take a Closer Look

1. You could lose your balance on a ladder and injure yourself with the saw.

2. A tree service can remove large branches safely in dangerous conditions.

Try It

1. Looks may not mean anything.
2. someone who can't find the flaws in a car

Use It

1. $1,005.01
2. It will continue to increase.

Lesson 25

Take a Closer Look

b

Try It

1. to stay cool
2. to stay warm

Use It

1. south
2. It is cold and makes travel difficult.

Lesson 26

Take a Closer Look

1. b   2. b

Try It

1. ways to plan for life
2. yes

Use It

1. They hear very well, at least high-pitched sounds.
2. They are different, and a bat can hear the difference.

Lesson 27

Take a Closer Look

b

Try It

1. the Grand Party
2. the New Party

Use It

1. Yes. Potatoes can be prepared in many ways and vary a great deal in shape and color.
2. Yes. Potatoes are rich in vitamin C and low in fat and calories.

Lesson 28

Take a Closer Look

1. one
2. no
3. no

Try It

1. It goes too far. The writer based it on only one bus route.
2. The buses on the C1 route are usually behind schedule.

Use It

1. It goes too far. The writer mentions only two experiences.
2. Some people treated me rudely.

Lesson 29

Take a Closer Look

Answers will vary.

Try It

Answers will vary.

Use It

Answers will vary.

Lesson 30

Take a Closer Look

1. an encyclopedia or atlas (and some dictionaries and almanacs)
2. probably not

Try It

1. in a dictionary
2. in an encyclopedia

Use It

1. in an encyclopedia
2. in magazines or newspapers

Lesson 31

Take a Closer Look

1. It should be built.
2. Answers will vary.

Try It

1. It should be postponed.
2. Answers will vary.

Use It

1. b
2. Answers will vary.